Homemade
Knit, Sew & Crochet
25 home craft projects

Ros Badger and Elspeth Thompson

Photography by Benjamin J Murphy

Collins

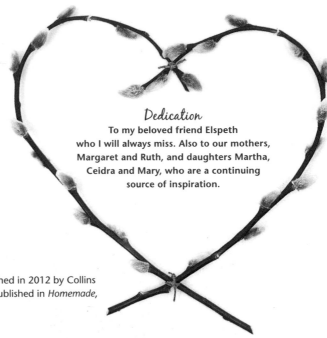

Dedication

To my beloved friend Elspeth
who I will always miss. Also to our mothers,
Margaret and Ruth, and daughters Martha,
Ceidra and Mary, who are a continuing
source of inspiration.

This paperback edition published in 2012 by Collins
includes some material first published in *Homemade*,
first published in 2009.

HarperCollins*Publishers*
77–85 Fulham Palace Road
London W6 8JB

www.harpercollins.co.uk

16 15 14 13 12

9 8 7 6 5 4 3 2 1

A catalogue record for this book is available from
the British Library.

ISBN: 978-000-748953-4

Photography Benjamin J Murphy

Editors Emma Callery and Sarah Tomley

Design Tracy Killick

Illustrations Mary Mathieson and Rosie Scott

Packager Tracy Killick Art Direction and Design

Printed and bound in China by South China
Printing Co Ltd

Contents

Introduction

There was a time, not so very long ago, when the term 'homemade' was synonymous with dowdiness and 'doing without'. From the profligate 1980s on, shopping seemed to become the preferred national pastime, while making your own was seen as second-best, an eccentricity, or a leftover from childhood TV programmes. But a few years ago a gradual shift began to occur. There was a revival of the old crafts combined with a new energetic approach. Knitting and crochet were suddenly in the zeitgeist and popular again, and everyone from New York bankers to teenage schoolgirls seemed to be starting crafts clubs.

Interest in craft has been growing among all sorts of groups and ages, and many people are now keen to make things for themselves, family and friends. The children's sewing club 'Sew Good', which I teach in the UK, has a long waiting list and I am inundated with people wanting to learn how to knit, sew and crochet. Many women now want to explore their creativity and make something stylish for the home, especially given the ever-growing interest in individual, handcrafted objects. My students are hugely diverse, from homemakers and business executives to children and other artisans. Recently an über-cool male student, studying Japanese, asked me to teach him how to crochet!

The 'homemade' movement has gained an added energy and momentum from the two major crises – environmental and financial – that now face us all. Making and growing

and one that I was lucky enough to turn into a career.

This book offers a range of stylish projects with something for everyone using a variety of skills, many requiring little experience. It does, however, require an alternative mindset to many craft books, which often start by listing stuff to buy, whereas I think half the fun lies in saving materials wherever you can, from fabric and buttons taken off favourite old clothes or furnishings, to ribbon from unwrapped presents. As these saved and salvaged materials become stitched and woven into new objects, the backdrop to our lives gathers texture and richness, with added layers of memory and association.

things not only saves money and helps the environment, the activities themselves give rise to a feel-good factor that can help cheer us up in adversity. Our homes become havens in times of global uncertainty, and knowing that we have the skills and resources to make things of use and beauty for those we live around and love – without costing the earth – can be a source of great comfort and pleasure.

My aims with this book are the same as they have always been – to spread the joy of creating and making things yourself, and to share that with others. Creating something is a satisfying and fulfilling thing to do and has been a constant in my life. Having been taught to crochet by my grandmother at the age of seven, I wore homemade clothes that my mother made for me as a child and then started to sew and knit my own designs as a teenager, not only because it was an economical way to live but because I was able to establish my individual style. This is still a vital part of my own creative process

I have always been proud to be seen as a creative person, but now we are firmly back to a time where craft is not the preserve of an envied talented few, but widespread across the globe. 'Homemade' (including 'homegrown') has become a way of life for a huge number of people. So many people can now be heard saying with pride, 'I made it myself!' People are no longer happy with doing the odd bit of knitting on their commuter train or taking a homemade gift to a party – they want to 'live the life', and embrace the authenticity and love behind everything homemade.

The increasing number of books, blogs and websites that have appeared over the last couple of years extolling the virtues of all things homemade give me hope that this wonderful trend is here to stay.

Ros Badger

iPod cover

Precious iPods look even better tucked inside gorgeous homemade covers. This pattern is simple enough for novice knitters, and can be customised by varying the colour or design in subtle or bold ways.

Tension over stocking stitch
16sts and 22 rows = 5cm (2in)

Abbreviations
See page 77

Measurements
7 x 8.5cm (2¾ x 3½in)

To make an iPod Nano cover
• With 2.75mm (UK size 12; US size 2) needles and the 4-ply cotton, cast on 22sts and work 8 rows in garter st (knit every row) then work in stocking st (knit one row, purl one row) until the cover measures 15cm (6in).

• Work 8 rows garter st and cast off.

• Fold the bag in half, right sides together, sew the two side seams and then turn through.

To make an iPod classic or other MP3 player cover
• Measure your player and, using the tension guide (see above), work out how many sts you need for the width, then add 4 more sts.

• With 2.75mm (UK size 12; US size 2) needles, cast on the required number of sts and work 8 rows garter st, then work in stocking st until the piece measures twice the length of your player. Work 8 more rows

of garter st and cast off. Fold the bag in half, right sides together, sew the two side seams and then turn through.

To make the strap
The simplest way to make a strap is to attach a colourful piece of ribbon. However, if you know how to crochet, the following instructions explain how to make a strong, pretty strap.

• With the 2.5mm crochet hook and 4-ply cotton, make a 30cm (12in) long single chain.

• Thread this through the knitted bag just below the garter st top. There is no need to make eyelet holes as the chain can easily be threaded through between the knitted sts. Tie together the loose ends to make a loop.

You will need
• 4-ply cotton, approximately 10g (½oz) (we used mercerised cotton, which has a slight sheen and washes well)

• 2.75mm (UK size 12; US size 2) knitting needles

• 2.5mm crochet hook (if making optional strap)

Tea cosy

As well as keeping your tea hot, a homemade tea cosy brings an air of warmth and originality to the kitchen table. Choose colours that work with your cups and kitchen décor.

You will need

- About 60g (2¼oz) yarn (this was knitted using Aran tweed but any Aran yarn would also work)
- Yarn scraps in contrasting colours for the embroidery and pompom
- 4.5mm (UK size 7; US size 7) needles (you can change the needle size to make the cosy larger or smaller; the one pictured fits a six-teacup teapot)

Tension
10sts and 12 rows = 5cm (2in)

Abbreviations
See page 77

To make
• With 4.5mm (UK size 7; US size 7) needles and yarn, cast on 84sts and work 5 rows to form the border.

Row 1: Knit.
Row 2: Purl.
Repeat these 2 rows once more then divide (work for spout and handle).

Row 5: K42 and keep remaining sts on a stitch holder.
Row 6: K2, p38, k2.
Repeat the last 2 rows 10 times more, ending on a purl row. Keep these sts on a stitch holder and repeat on the opposite side until the work measures the same front and back. End on a purl row.
Next row: Knit across the whole work.
Next row: Purl.

Then start decreasing as follows:
Row 1: K11, k2tog, * k12, k2tog*, repeat from * to * 5 times, k1. (78sts)
Row 2: Purl.
Row 3: K10, k2tog, * k11, k2tog*, repeat from * to * 5 times, k1. (72sts)
Row 4: Purl.
Row 5: K9, k2tog, * k10, k2tog*, repeat from * to * 5 times, k1. (66sts)
Row 6: Purl.
Row 7: K8, k2tog, * k9, k2tog*, repeat from * to * 5 times, k1. (60sts)
Row 8: Purl.
Row 9: K7, k2tog, * k8, k2tog*, repeat from * to * 5 times, k1. (54sts)
Row 10: Purl.
Row 11: K6, k2tog, * k7, k2tog*, repeat from * to * 5 times, k1. (48sts)
Row 12: Purl.

Row 13: K1, k2tog across work to the last st, k1. 27sts remain.

• Cut your thread and then thread it through all the sts, pulling it tightly.

• Use this thread to sew the side seam as far as the opening for the spout, where the 2-st garter st edging finishes.

• Sew the bottom side seam to where the 2-st garter st edging begins.

• Work your motif (here, a teacup; see pattern on page 85) using chain st (see page 73) and a contrasting colour of wool.

• Tack the shape first, if you like, working out from the centre of the tea cosy to ensure the motif is central. Work a box in running st (see page 74) around the image in a contrasting colour of wool.

• Make a pompom (see pages 12–13) and attach securely to the top.

Pompoms

Pompoms can be used in all sorts of fun and stylish ways; they lend a jaunty air to clothing and furnishings. Tie them to lengths of twisted wool to make attractive drawstrings for clothes, bags or gloves.

You will need

- Cardboard circles. Decide what size pompoms you would like, then for each pompom cut two cardboard circles with that diameter. Cut out a smaller circle in the centre (to the proportions shown in the photograph, right)

- Darning needle or bobbin

- Yarn

To make

- With the yarn threaded through a large darning needle or bobbin, wind it all around the doughnut shape, tightly and thickly.

- When the cardboard is covered and you can hardly get your needle through the central hole, cut the yarn all around the outer edge of the circle and secure by tying another piece of yarn tightly around the centre of the pompom.

- Remove the cardboard and fluff up the pompom. Trim with a pair of sharp scissors to even it up into a perfect ball. This can also help the edges of the yarn to fluff up nicely.

- Attach your pompom securely with matching yarn to whatever you are making.

Striped woolly scarf

This is just about the most simple scarf ever – and it looks great on men, women and children. Use contrasting colours for the cast-on and cast-off edge to add an attractive finish.

You will need

- 200g (7oz) chunky yarn in main colour (MC) – we used duck-egg blue
- Approximately 30g (1¼oz) chunky yarn in colour B (col B) – we used orange
- Approximately 30g (1¼oz) chunky yarn in colour C (col C) – we used green
- 6.5mm (UK size 3; US size 10½) knitting needles

Tension over garter stitch

The yarn we used worked out at the following tension, but note the needle size and tension on your ball of wool (usually written on the ball band) in case it is different, and change accordingly.

14sts and 26 rows = 10cm (4in)

Abbreviations

See page 77

Measurements

22 x 115cm (8½ x 45in)

To make

- With 6.5mm needles (UK size 3; US size 10½) and col B, cast on 30sts.

Rows 1–4: Change to col C, knit.
Rows 5 & 6: Col B, knit.
Rows 7 & 8: MC, knit.
Rows 9 & 10: Col C, knit.
Rows 11 & 12: MC, knit.
Rows 13–16: Col B, knit.
Rows 17 & 18: Col C, knit.
Rows 19–22: MC, knit.
Rows 23 & 24: Col B, knit.
Rows 25 & 26: Col C, knit.
Rows 27–44: MC, knit.
Rows 45 & 46: Col B, knit.
Rows 47–52: MC, knit.
Rows 53 & 54: Col C, knit.
Rows 55–206: MC, knit.
Rows 207 & 208: Col C, knit.
Rows 209–214: MC, knit.
Rows 215 & 216: Col B, knit.
Rows 217–234: MC, knit.
Rows 235 & 236: Col C, knit.
Row 237–238: Col B, knit.
Rows 239–242: MC, knit.
Rows 243 & 244: Col C, knit.
Rows 245–248: Col B, knit.
Rows 249 & 250: MC, knit.
Rows 251 & 252: Col C, knit.
Rows 253 & 254: MC, knit.
Rows 255 & 256: Col B, knit.
Rows 257–260: Col C, knit.
Change to col B and cast off.
Weave in any loose ends.

- For a longer or shorter scarf, add or reduce rows between rows 55 and 206.

Tip

If you're looking for a great way to use up scraps of wool, incorporate lots of colour changes into your scarf. Just make sure that they are all of the same weight.

Fingerless gloves

These stripy gloves are warm and stylish but leave your fingers free.
You can make them shorter by reducing the number of rows between
rows 33 and 47, or longer by knitting extra rows before decreasing.

Abbreviations
See page 77

Tension
14sts and 18 rows = 5cm (2in)

Measurements
Finished length is approximately 26cm (10¼in)

Continues on page 19

You will need

- 25g (1oz) of 4-ply wool in colour A (col A) – we used brown
- 25g (1oz) of 4-ply wool in colour B (col B) – we used aubergine
- 25g (1oz) of 4-ply wool in colour C (col C) – we used moss
- 3.25mm (UK size 10; US size 3) knitting needles

It would be very easy to knit rainbow stripes from this pattern if you have a range of colours to hand.

To make the right glove

• With 3.25mm (UK size 10; US size 3) needles and col B, cast on 59sts.
Change to col A and work 6 rows in k1, p1 rib.
Dec 1st at end of row 6. (58sts) (For decreasing, knit together the 3rd and 4th sts from the edge. This produces a fashioning mark on the gloves, which gives them a more stylish finish.)
Cont with col A.
Row 1 (RS): Knit.
Row 2: Purl.
Row 3: Using col B, knit.
Row 4: Purl.
Row 5: Using col C, knit.
Row 6: Purl.
These 6 rows form the pattern.

Cont in pattern for stripes, dec 1st at each end of the following row and then on rows 15, 21, 27 and 33, until 48sts remain.

Cont until the beginning of row 47, then work thumb gusset as follows, keeping stripes correct.
Row 1 (RS): K24, inc in next st, k2, inc in next st, k20. (50sts)
Work 3 rows.
Row 5: K24, inc in next st, k4, inc in next st, k20. (52sts)
Work 3 rows.
Row 9: K24, inc in next st, k6, inc in next st, k20. (54sts)
Work 3 rows.
Row 13: K24, inc in next st, k8, inc in next st, k20. (56sts)
Work 3 rows.
Row 17: K24, inc in next st, k10, inc in next st, k20. (58sts)
Work 1 row.
Row 19: K38, turn and cast on 1st.

Row 20*: p14, turn and cast on 1st. (15sts)
Work 6 rows on these 15sts, keeping stripes correct.

Change to col A and work 2 rows in k1, p1 rib.
Cast off with col B.
Join the thumb seam.
With right sides facing, rejoin yarn, pick up 4sts from the thumb base (2 either side of seam) and cont to end of row.
Work 16 rows more.
Change to col A and work 4 rows in k1, p1 rib.
Change to col B and cast off.

To make the left glove

• Work as right glove to the beginning of thumb gusset shaping. Then work as follows:
Row 1 (RS): K19, inc in next st, k2, inc in next st, k25. (50sts)
Work 3 rows.
Row 5: K19, inc in next st, k4, inc in next st, k25. (52sts)
Work 3 rows.
Row 9: K19, inc in next st, k6, inc in next st, k25. (54sts)
Work 3 rows.
Row 13: K19, inc in next st, k8, inc in next st, k25. (56sts)
Work 3 rows.
Row 17: K19, inc in next st, k10, inc in next st, k25. (58sts)
Work 1 row.
Row 19: K33, turn and cast on 1st, cont as for right glove from *.

Making up

• Sew the side seam with mattress stitch, catching in ends where you can. Then sew in any remaining ends and press lightly with your iron on the wool setting.

Felt flower hair clips and combs

These charming felt hair accessories are fun and fashionable, and they are simple enough for children to make. They make great presents or items to sell at a school fair.

You will need

- Scraps of felt in contrasting colours
- Cotton thread in matching colours
- Hair clip
- Undecorated hair comb

To make the flowers

- Cut a strip of felt approximately 10 x 1.5–2.5cm (4 x ½–1in), depending on how large you want your flowers. Cut one edge with pinking shears, then use standard scissors to cut between each 'v' of the pinked edge to approximately 5mm (¼in) from the opposite edge.

- For the flower centre, cut a piece of felt in a contrasting colour 50 x 5mm (2 x ¼in). Roll it up to form the centre of your flower and then roll the petal strip around it, sewing the edges and underside securely to hold it all together.

- For a simple hair clip, use just one or two flowers. If making a comb slide, make five in various colours and sizes (see opposite). Then progress as follows.

To make the comb

- Cut a piece of felt the width of the comb and 2cm (¾in) high (or double the height of the top of the comb). Stitch the felt onto the top of the comb, sewing between each tooth and neatly finishing at the ends. Sew five flowers in a random order onto the felt edge of your comb, stitching from the underneath (where it will not show).

To make the hair clip

- Cut a leaf shape in double-thickness felt, then sew around the edge with running stitch. Sew a line down the centre to form the leaf vein. Stitch your flower to one end of the leaf and then sew the leaf to a hair clip, securing it in three places by sewing over the straight edge of the clip and the underside of the leaf using a small over stitch.

Tip

Add texture by inserting narrow strips of felt, looped between the flowers, or add a few small, green leaves.

Flower corsage

Fabric corsages add instant glamour to a party dress or a plain top. This corsage is simple to make and can be given endless variations by using different colours and textures, and old or new fabrics.

You will need

- Scraps of fabric in contrasting materials, colours and patterns (you need at least five different fabric scraps to build a flower)
- Cotton thread for hand or machine sewing (we used silver thread)
- Brooch pin (optional)

To make

- Cut various size circles of fabrics and layer them five or six deep, using a variety of different thicknesses and textures, such as velvet and net. Use pinking shears to cut the edges of some fabrics, to give added interest around the edge.

- Sew four lines across the diameter of the circles to divide each circle into eight segments, using machine or hand stitching. We used silver thread, which seems to look pretty with everything. Leave loose strands of thread at the edges of the flower by not trimming too close – this adds to the overall effect.

- Cut from the outside to the inside of each flower, between the lines of stitching, to a point just short of the centre. Then turn over the corsage and pinch together each segment near the centre (see below left), then sew around your pinch, drawing the thread slightly tight to pull the flower into a three-dimensional shape.

- Sew the finished corsage firmly into place on your chosen piece of clothing or a bag. If you want to be able to transfer the corsage from garment to garment, attach a brooch pin to the back.

Tip

A group of corsages would look great on a belt or waistband – and they can even be used to hide the odd worn patch or moth hole on a much-loved cashmere jersey.

Bag-in-a-bag

Plastic carrier bags are a definite no-no for style and eco reasons. This homemade replacement is strong enough to carry lots of heavy groceries, light enough to fit in your handbag, and über-stylish.

To make

• To make the bag, cut out a rectangular piece of fabric that measures 80 x 46cm (32 x 18in). This includes a 1.5cm (½in) seam allowance.

• To make the straps, cut two strips of fabric, each measuring 54 x 9cm (21 x 3½in). Fold in 5mm (¼in) on each side to the wrong side and iron flat. Then fold each strap in half lengthways (so that the pattern is on the outside and the folded edges are facing inwards), and machine topstitch all the way along.

• For the top edge of the bag, fold in one of the longer sides of the main piece of fabric by 3mm (⅛in) to the wrong side.

Iron in place and then fold down a further 4cm (1½in) and iron again.

• Pin the two handles in place. Pin one end of the first handle about 10cm (4in) in from the right-side edge, then pin the other end about 13cm (5in) away from the first. Make sure the stitches on the handles face inward, and that the bottom of each handle is level with the bottom of the folded-over edge of the bag (see page 27, top right). Repeat at the opposite end (starting 10cm/4in) from the left-side edge) for handle two.

Continues on page 27

• With the handles in place, stitch down the top of the bag with two rows of machine stitching, one about 3mm (¹/₈in) from the top edge and the other along the bottom of the folded-over edge (see top right).

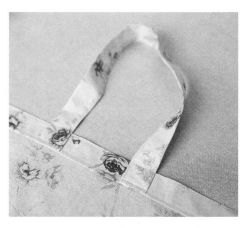

• Fold the bag in half, right sides together. Sew the side and bottom seams about 1.5cm (½in) in from the edge. Zigzag stitch over the raw edges to prevent fraying.

• To make the gusset, open the bag out so the bottom seam runs down the centre and sew a diagonal line of about 10cm (4in) across each corner (see below right).

• To make the ribbon and button tie, loop the length of ribbon around one of the handles, joining and securing with a button (see left).

• To pack away the bag, fold it into three or four sections and roll up, leaving the straps end until last. Then simply wrap the ribbon tie around the roll and wind the loose end of the ribbon around the button to secure.

Beach bag

This good-looking, roomy bag has been designed to carry everything you need for the beach, from lotions to lunch. Its towelled lining means even wet swimsuits and goggles are no problem.

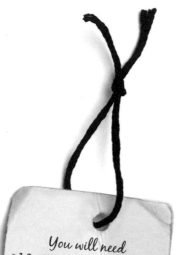

To make

• For the bag, cut two pieces measuring 115 x 50cm (45 x 20in): one from the main fabric and the other from towelling. Place the wrong sides together and use as a single piece, tacking together if necessary.

• For the straps, cut two strips of the main fabric, each measuring 95 x 10cm (27½ x 4in).

• Make up the bag using the instructions for the Bag-in-a-bag on pages 24–27.

• To decorate, stitch an anchor (see page 85) or other seaside image onto your bag using chain stitch (see page 73). We used tapestry wool rather than embroidery thread because wool really stands out, and then we added a rope-like piece of trimming recycled from a carrier bag. You could add shells and other beachcombing finds, strung like fashionable chains or trophies from the straps.

You will need

• 1.2m (4ft) in any standard width of strong cotton or canvas-type fabric (we used gingham), or use an off-cut measuring 115 x 70cm (45 x 28in)

• Towelling: same size as the main fabric – an old towel would be perfect

• Cotton thread for machine sewing

• Tapestry wool

• Recycled rope, shells and anything else you have to hand, to decorate

Child's summer dress

With simple, classic childrenswear back in fashion, frocks such as this cost the earth in shops but they are not difficult to make. This pattern can be made up in two sizes – for a one- or a three-year-old.

To make

• Cut out the dress pieces as directed on the pattern pieces on pages 82–84, placing the front and back skirt pieces and bodice front against a fold of fabric. We have allowed a 1cm (½in) seam throughout. For the bodice, cut two pieces each of front and back, one of fabric and one of lining. Cut two sashes (optional). With right sides facing, pin the left shoulder seam of the bodice and sew. Repeat with the bodice lining, sewing the left shoulder seam.

• With right sides together, pin the main bodice fabric to the lining, matching up the sewn left shoulder seam. Sew around the left armhole. Then, beginning at the bottom of the right armhole, sew around the back of the right armhole, around the neck – back and front – and around the front of the right armhole.

• Trim the seams using sharp scissors and clip around the curved edges to help the bodice lie flat when turned. (You can also machine around the seams using a zigzag stitch to prevent the seams fraying.) Turn to the right side by pulling the front through at the left shoulder. Iron the seams flat.

• For the sashes, if using, fold the sash pieces in half lengthways, right sides together. Sew around the two sides, allowing for a 1cm (½in) seam. Trim the corners, then turn to the right side using a knitting needle, if necessary, to push out the corners. Press with a steam iron.

Continues on page 33

• Pin the sashes to the front side seam of the bodice, matching the raw edge of the sash to the side of the bodice, approximately 2cm (¾in) from the bottom edge.

• Place the front and back pieces right sides together and matching the underarm seam. Sew the lining side seam, across the underarm seam and then the bodice seam, which catches in the sash. Repeat on the opposite side.

• Make a horizontal buttonhole on the back right shoulder, to fit your button (see pages 74–75). Sew either on the sewing machine or by hand with blanket stitch (see page 73). Sew the button onto the back shoulder.

• To make up the skirt, stitch the front to the back side seams. Then make two parallel rows of gathering stitches (long running stitches, see page 74) at the top edge on the front and back to within 1cm (½in) of the side seams. Pull gently to make the gathers the same width as the bodice.

• With right sides together, matching side seams with the side seams from the main fabric only, tack the two pieces of the dress together, then sew on or just below the gathering stitches. Trim and finish the join between bodice and skirt with zigzag stitch and press the seam upwards.

• Press under the raw edge of the bodice lining by about 1cm (½in) and hand sew with over stitch (see page 74) the folded edge below the stitched line of the gathered skirt to bodice, so hiding the stitch line. Press with a steam iron.

• Mark the finished length and trim evenly, allowing about 2cm (¾in) to turn up and press all around. Then press under approximately 5mm (¼in) along the raw edge and stitch the hem either by hand or by machine.

Tips

Use a contrasting or coordinating fabric for the bodice lining and choose a colourful button from your button tin for the shoulder strap to make your dress unique. The pieces of fabric are so small that you could cut them from an item of adult clothing – a favourite old skirt, for instance – that is worn in patches but still has large areas of strong, pretty fabric.

We both grew up wearing pretty floral dresses like this. They have now become a tradition, handmade with love in summer and winter versions.

Patchwork throw

Patchwork is as fiddly as you want to make it. The modern 'cheat's' approach is to machine-sew together fragments of fabric to form a flat piece of material for making clothes or furnishings.

You will need

- Assorted pieces of denim, ticking and tea towels
- Cotton thread for machine sewing
- Old sheet, blanket or length of fabric

To make

- Choose which pieces of fabric you are going to work with. Look for a good distribution of colours, stripes and textures throughout, and make sure you have enough – it will always show if you run out towards the end and have to introduce new material.

- Cut strips and squares of random length but more or less the same width – here they are 15–20cm (6–8in). On the throw shown in the photograph, the stripes face the same way on alternating pieces. If you want to do the same thing, divide your fabric into two equal piles and arrange them so that the stripes are vertical for one half and horizontal for the other.

- The idea is to first sew the pieces into long strips (as long as you need to stretch over your chair or sofa), and then to machine them together to form a large piece of fabric. Start by sewing together a line of pieces in a well-spaced yet random-looking order, with all the stripes facing the appropriate direction. Do this several times, until you have enough to join them up and form the throw.

- Pin or tack the strips together, with stripes facing upwards one row, crossways on the next. Machine stitch together.

- Trim the seams, trimming away large overlaps where necessary, and iron the fabric into shape.

- Make a backing for the patchwork using an old sheet, blanket, canvas or something similar, using contrasting or coordinating colours. Cut this to the same size as the patchwork piece. Place right sides together then machine around the edge, as if making a huge cushion, leaving a little gap along one edge. Turn right sides out through this gap, sew up and iron into shape. With any leftover fabric, make a couple of cushion covers to match.

Tip

This is a great way to use the good parts of jeans too worn to wear, or the unsullied borders of singed or stained tea towels, which can be picked up cheaply in second-hand shops.

Cushion covers

Why buy expensive cushion covers when they are dead easy to make and a great way to use up odd pieces of fabric? Part of the fun lies in choosing and matching the materials.

You will need

- New or vintage fabric such as an old silk scarf, worn linen curtains, or something woolly, like an old blanket or a large much-loved sweater
- Cushion pad
- Wool for blanket stitch (optional)
- Buttons or tapes for opening (optional)

To make

• Cut a length of fabric two-and-a-half times longer than your cushion pad, plus 2.5cm (1in) all around to allow for seams. If there is a stripe or pattern in the fabric, work out where you would like this on the cushion before you start cutting.

• Hem any unfinished edges or fold over and edge with blanket stitch (see page 73).

• Fold the fabric, right sides together, as if wrapping around a cushion, so that the edge you want visible for the outer side of the envelope comes two-thirds of the way up the length of the cushion. Make sure, too, that this edge is inside, facing downwards, with the other flap over the top.

• Machine or hand stitch securely along the two outside edges of the cover, sewing through two and then three layers of fabric. Turn the cover inside out, iron if required and insert the cushion pad.

• Sew on buttons or tapes to fasten the opening, if required. See page 74 for instructions on making a buttonhole.

Using a contrasting colour or texture for each side can look very stylish. Try mixing knitted cotton or linen with a woven linen stripe, felted cashmere with slub silk, or even suede with sheepskin or sequins.

Outdoor cushion

Give old garden seating a lift with smart, tie-on fabric cushions. Choose a hardwearing material and remember that a mismatch of vintage fabrics looks lovely, so raid your scrap box for possibilities.

You will need

- Cushion pad or thick foam cut to size
- Hardwearing fabric, such as canvas, striped ticking or oilcloth
- Sewing thread to match fabric
- 80cm (32in) tape or ribbon

To make

- This cushion has an envelope-style opening like the one on pages 36–37. Cut three pieces of fabric: one the size of your cushion plus a 2cm (¾in) seam allowance (Piece A); and two that each measure two-thirds of the length of the cushion plus seam allowance (Pieces B and C). Pieces B and C will ultimately overlap each other on the back of the cushion to form the opening for inserting the pad. You may want to cut out Piece C with the selvedge forming the open edge.

- Hem the unfinished edge of B that will form part of the opening (and C, too, if you haven't made use of the selvedge).

- Cut four lengths of tape or ribbon 20cm (8in) long each for the ties.

- Lay out your pieces with Piece A on the bottom (right side facing up), followed by Pieces B and then C on top (right sides facing down) so that they overlap, pinning two ties between the layers of fabric at each of the two adjacent corners so that the ends of the ties are trapped between the seams.

- Sew around the four sides. Turn the cushion cover out so the right side is visible, iron the seams flat, insert the cushion pad and use the ties to attach to the back of the chair.

Denim chair

Old denim jeans are great for patchwork, as the flies, pockets and worn and faded patches all add interest. This director's chair looks complicated but is actually very easy to make.

You will need

- A director's chair that has seen better days
- Sandpaper and wood treatment (optional)
- Pair of old denim jeans or denim off-cuts
- Cotton thread for machine sewing
- Hammer and nails or staple gun

To make

- Remove the sling seat and back from an old director's chair and keep as a pattern piece. If the wood is worn or stained you can sand it down and, if necessary, re-varnish at this stage.

- Cut up the denim jeans or off-cuts into pieces that are a similar width but of varying lengths. Stitch them together to make two flat pieces of fabric, each roughly the size of the seat and back pieces you have removed. Allow 2cm (¾in) extra at the top and bottom edges to hem and at least 8cm (3¼in) at the sides for attaching to the chair frame. The easiest way to make the denim patchwork is to use a sewing machine to sew pieces into several long strips and then to sew these together. Trim the seams to neaten.

- When deciding which piece of fabric is going where, keep in mind where interesting features on the jeans will appear on the finished chair – we used the fly detail for the back and a pair of pockets for the seat. Make sure the seat, in particular, is made from strong, unworn pieces, as it will be carrying the most weight when in use.

- Turn over the top and bottom edges of each patchworked piece and hem by hand or machine, using the original seat covers as a guide.

- Wrap the edges around the chair frame so that the raw edges are hidden, and then nail or staple the back and seat securely into place.

Tip

Cutting up a pair of jeans and sewing the bits together to make a flat piece of fabric can be the basic starting point for any number of projects, from cushion covers to simple upholstery.

Summer bunting

Strung from leafy branches and blowing gently in a warm breeze, fabric bunting brings a festive air to the summer garden. Good times are here, it seems to say, suggesting parties and wholesome fun and games.

You will need

- A mixture of plain, striped and floral cotton fabrics (fabric scraps or swatches need to be at least 22cm [8½in] square)
- 16m (17½yd) coloured tape or binding a minimum of 2cm (¾in) wide
- Cotton thread for machine sewing

To make

• Using pinking shears (so that you don't have to hem each piece), cut out 50 triangles, each measuring 22cm (8½in) wide and deep. Decide on the order of your coloured triangles, aiming to get a good mix of patterns and colours.

• Fold the tape in half lengthways and iron it to make a long channel for inserting the triangles.

• Starting about 20cm (8in) in from the end of the tape (to leave some free for tying), pin the triangles in position, 10cm (4in) apart, opening up the tape and slipping the top of each triangle inside so the raw edge is hidden. Stop 20cm (8in) short of the other end of the tape.

• Machine carefully into place all along the length of the tape to secure the triangles.

• Making a loop at either end can make hanging easier, and extra tape can be added to extend the bunting or to make it easier to tie onto trees and so on.

Tips

Bunting looks beautiful indoors as well as out, looped along verandahs, draped across doorways or hung in swags around the walls of a child's bedroom year-round. This bunting is machine-washable and is best kept folded flat in a box between uses to prevent it getting tangled.

Tea towel apron

Some tea towels seem too good for wiping dishes, so why not make one into an apron? This idea is simplicity itself, as it utilises the ready-finished edges of the tea towel, so there's hardly any hemming.

You will need

- Large tea towel measuring 62 x 84cm (24½ x 33in) for an average-sized adult. Use a smaller-sized one for a child
- White cotton thread
- 2.7m (3yd) cotton tape
- Metal D-ring (optional)

To make

• Cut off the top corners of your tea towel so that when sewn together along their diagonal sides, they form a square. Tea towels vary in size, but for this one, the cuts were made 18cm (7in) in along the top and down each side, leaving 27cm (10½in) (unhemmed) for the neckline.

• Turn over the raw edges of the main tea towel twice, press with a steam iron and hem by hand.

• To make the pocket, tack together the diagonal sides of the two cut-off triangles, right sides facing, making sure to match any stripes or patterns where you can. Carefully machine stitch together.

• Iron out the seam, fold over the raw edges of the pocket square once and hand hem the one that will form the top of the pocket. Pin or tack the pocket into position on the front of the apron and top stitch by machine, finishing securely at all the corners.

• To finish, cut the cotton tape into three: two ties of 106cm (42in) each and a neck loop of 60cm (24in). Sew securely into position, using the metal D-ring to make the neck loop adjustable, if required. Press with a steam iron.

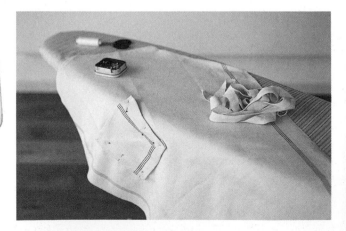

Egg cosies

These colourful egg cosies will cheer up your breakfast table as well as keeping your eggs warm. Simple enough for small children to make under adult supervision, they also make great Easter presents.

You will need
- Pieces of felt and leftover scraps in different colours
- Sewing thread in various colours to contrast with the felt

To make the chicken cosy (opposite)

• Using the chicken pattern on page 80, cut out two pieces for the body and, in a contrasting colour, another two pieces for the wings. Pin a wing to each chicken shape and sew the rounded end of the wings to the chicken's body using over stitch (see page 74).

• Make the eyes by stitching a star shape on each chicken piece in the middle of the head. Alternatively, sew a button on either side.

• Place the chicken pieces wrong sides together and pin to hold. Then sew around the chickens from the bottom right-hand corner to the bottom left-hand corner with blanket stitch, or running stitch if preferred (see pages 73–74). In a different colour, work blanket stitch along the bottom edge.

To make the simple cosy (below left)

• Using the simple egg cosy pattern on page 80, cut out three pieces of felt in contrasting colours.

• Using scrap pieces of felt, decorate each piece with a motif of your choice. We cut out a flower for one of the cosies (you might choose to use the pattern on page 80) and letters for another (for example, 'EGG', or 'DAD'). Sew on the motifs with running stitch.

• Pin together two pieces of the cosy with wrong sides facing and sew along the seam with over stitch in a contrasting colour of thread. Add the third piece and sew along the remaining seams with over stitch.

Tip
Small items such as this offer good ways of using up odd pieces of felt and thread.

Hot-water bottle cover

This cosy hot-water bottle cover is a clever way to make use of an old jersey and it's an improvement on shop-bought versions, as it opens at the bottom so it won't be damaged by having to stretch over the stopper.

You will need

- Large piece of paper
- Old jersey, preferably in soft cashmere or felted wool to avoid the pieces unravelling as you work
- Cotton thread to match jersey colour

To make

- Draw around your hot-water bottle, adding 1.5cm (½in) all around for a seam allowance. Then make two paper pattern pieces as follows:

Piece A: this must be at least 5cm (2in) longer than Piece B and incorporate the natural edge of the jersey at the bottom.

Piece B needs to be approximately 1cm (½in) shorter than the hot-water bottle.

Cutting the pattern pieces to these dimensions allows for the longer piece (A) to overlap the base of the bottle and also the shorter piece (B), creating the envelope opening.

- Cut out the two pattern pieces from your fabric, being sure to place the bottom edge of each pattern piece along the natural edge of the knitting.

- Fold up the bottom 5cm (2in) of Piece A, right side to right side, and pin or tack in place at the edges. Then, with right sides facing, place together the two pieces, matching up the tops. Piece B should be about 1cm (½in) shorter than Piece A.

- Sew around the cover using a small zigzag stitch on a sewing machine or use back stitch (see page 73) if sewing by hand. Do not sew along the folded edge.

- Turn right sides out and bring the 5cm (2in) fold to the front to create the envelope edge that secures your hot-water bottle in place.

Tip

This cover looks and feels good made out of old blankets too.

Lavender cats

Lavender bags have a somewhat quaint, old-fashioned image but there's every reason to update them, because they will make your drawers or car smell absolutely gorgeous, and they make lovely gifts.

You will need

- Dried lavender or fresh lavender for drying at home
- Plain cotton fabric (an old sheet is fine)
- Fabric paints and crayons
- Paintbrushes
- Cotton thread for machine or hand sewing

To dry lavender

- If you have lavender in your garden, you can dry your own flowers. Harvesting just as the top florets are opening ensures the strongest scent, but after flowering, when the blooms are already drying on the stems, is also fine. Cut the flowers with long stems and tie with string into bunches of 30 or so stems. Place the head of each bunch in a brown paper bag, tie up with string and hang, flowers downwards, in a dry place for ten days to two weeks. When the flowers are fully dry, open the bags and pull off any remaining florets that have not fallen from the stems.

To make the fabric cat

- Transfer the cat pattern on page 81 onto a piece of cotton fabric folded into two. Cut around the design, leaving 1cm (½in) all around as a seam allowance. Paint the pieces of fabric with fabric paints or crayons. Iron to fix the design according to product instructions on your fabric paints or crayons.

- Turn right sides together and machine or hand sew around the outline, leaving a gap of about 5cm (2in) along the bottom edge for stuffing. Snip in towards the seam on the curved edges so the bag will lie flat when opened out.

- Turn right sides out and iron into shape, using the pointed ends of scissors to push out any awkward corners. Stuff with dried lavender – or lavender mixed with small dried beans (such as mung beans) to add weight – and then neatly hand sew up the opening. Make sure not to get the lavender cat wet, especially if beans have been included.

Tips

These hand-painted lavender cats were made by our friend the artist Mary Mathieson (see Directory, page 90). They can be made in any size – tiny ones for tucking into drawers to keep clothes fresh and protect against moths, or large enough to double up as fragrant cushions. You could personalise the cats by painting or sewing on a name.

Victorian sand pincushion

The Victorians made decorated pincushions to commemorate births, weddings and other significant occasions. We've revived the idea but brought it up to date with a simplified design.

You will need

- Scraps of plain velvet or similar fabric
- Cotton thread for machine sewing
- 1.2kg (2½lb) sand for a cushion measuring 18 x 16cm (7 x 6¼in)
- Tissue paper (optional)
- 1 pack of dressmaker's or diamanté-style pins

To make

• Cut out two pieces of fabric each measuring approximately 18 x 16cm (7 x 6¼in). Place right sides together and machine sew around the edges with very small stitches so the sand cannot find a way out, leaving a small gap on one edge. If you're worried about sand leaking out, you could make an inner bag of the same size in calico or fine cotton.

• Trim the corner seams, turn the bag right sides out, iron into shape and fill tightly with sand. Sew up the opening neatly.

• Decide on your design. Work freehand from a drawing or sketch it out on tissue paper, pinning the paper in place and working your design through the paper onto the cushion.

• Begin sticking in your pins to create the design, working methodically from the middle out, to ensure symmetry. If you have used tissue paper, tear it away once the design is complete.

Tips

Use play sand from a children's store for a clean, hygienic sand. Be sure to keep the pincushion well away from small children, to whom the pins could be harmful. Diamanté-style pins add a luxurious touch.

Cross-stitch 'no-entry' sign

Cross stitch is often associated with old-fashioned samplers,
and you can easily make your own versions to celebrate a birth or marriage.
But why not give cross stitch a contemporary twist with a simple graphic?

You will need

- Two pieces of aida (also known as binka): 8-count for larger stitches, 16-count for smaller, finer ones
- Embroidery thread
- Embroidery needle
- Embroidery hoop (optional)

To make

- Draw a circle with a line diagonally through the centre onto one piece of your aida (cross-stitch fabric). If you're a beginner, ask for a low-count aida cloth, such as 8 – this means the fabric will only require 8 stitches per inch, whereas 16-count requires much smaller stitches, fitting 16 of them into one inch.

- Cross stitch the pattern in red embroidery thread, if you want to follow convention, or use a colour suited to wherever you're thinking of hanging the sign. Divide the 6 threads of your embroidery thread in half, so you stitch with 3 threads. If you have an embroidery hoop it will make life much easier, but don't worry if you don't have access to one.

- Begin stitching at the centre of the diagonal line, stitching out to the circle and around it, then back to the centre.

- Take the two pieces of fabric, turn right sides together and machine or hand sew around the edge, leaving a gap of about 5cm (2in) along the bottom edge for stuffing. Snip in towards the seam on the curved edges so the aida bag will lie flat when opened out.

- Turn right sides out and iron into shape, using the pointed ends of scissors to push out any awkward corners. Stuff with dried lavender (see page 51) or hops. Add some dried beans or rice if you want the sign to have more weight.

Tip

Try using upholstery fabric or cotton velvet for the back of your sign for added textural interest.

Crochet squares

Like knitting, crochet has lost its former fuddy-duddy image to become highly fashionable, with designers such as Dolce & Gabbana and Vivienne Westwood sending crocheted dresses and accessories down the catwalks in recent years. Luckily, it is even easier than knitting to learn and can become quite addictive! Crochet squares, joined together in a funky-coloured patchwork, are a perennial favourite – and are also the simplest and easiest way to start. Once you have mastered the basic square, several can be joined together to make anything from a simple scarf or cushion cover to a large double blanket like this one.

Traditionally a way of using up scraps of leftover yarn, patchwork crochet has to be carefully planned if it is not to end up looking a disordered mess. This blanket, bought in a thrift shop, was made in the 1940s by someone who clearly had a keen sense of colour and design. Though each square is random in colour and order for the first three rounds (rings of crocheting, starting in the middle of the square, see page 59), it is coordinated with the surrounding squares for the final, outer round – a brown marl for the squares that make up the central panel, then apple green, and finishing with blue for the wide surround that hangs down the bed.

This simple discipline really draws the design together – if you look carefully you can see squares using the same or similar colours distributed irregularly but reasonably evenly throughout the blanket. A similar effect could be achieved by working out which yarn you have most of and using it to work the outer round of each of your squares.

Turn the page for instructions to start making your very own family heirloom.

Abbreviations
See page 79

To make a single crochet square

• This is an easy, basic square for anyone who can crochet. For a good introduction to basic crochet skills, see the courses listed in the Directory on pages 88–89. The following makes a square measuring approximately 7.5cm (3in). Work each round in a different colour yarn.

• With a 3.25mm crochet hook and yarn, make 6ch. Join in a circle with a sl st.

Round 1: 5ch (count as 1tr and 2ch), 11tr into centre, sl st to 3rd of 5ch.
Round 2: Sl st into next ch, 5ch (count as 1tr and 3ch), 3tr into same space, *1ch, miss 3tr (3tr, 2ch, 3tr) into next sp, repeat from * twice, 1ch, miss 3sts, 2tr into same sp as 5ch at beginning of round, sl st to 3rd of 5ch.
Round 3: Sl st into next ch, 5ch (count as 1tr and 2ch), 3tr into same sp, *1ch, miss 3tr, 3tr into next sp, 1ch, miss 3tr **, (3tr, 2ch, 3tr) into next sp, repeat from * twice, and from * to ** again, 2tr into same sp as 5ch, sl st to 3rd of 5ch.
Round 4: Sl st into next ch, 5ch (count as 1tr and 2ch), 3tr into same space, * (1ch, miss 3tr, 3tr into next sp) twice, 1ch, miss 3tr **, (3tr, 2ch, 3tr) into next sp, repeat from * twice, and from * to ** again, 2tr into same sp as 5ch, sl st to 3rd of 5ch.
Fasten off.

Making up a blanket

• Work as many squares as possible, thinking about your palette as discussed on the previous page. Join your squares together with dc by placing squares wrong sides together. Join all squares with the same colour throughout the blanket, keeping some aside for repairs.

• When all the squares are joined together, work a border around the edge in the following way:

Round 1: Work 3tr 1ch into each space between 3trs of each square edge.
Rounds 2 to 4: Work 1dc into each tr all around blanket.
Fasten off.

• The border can be worked in a plain colour or in different colours for each round, depending on the effect you want and how much yarn you have left.

Crochet bowls

These useful crochet bowls are perfect for keeping lots of small objects in one place. They are quick and easy to make, and sit prettily on tables or can be tucked into drawers to tidy away make-up or trinkets.

You will need
- 1 x 25g (1oz) double-knit cotton yarn
- 3mm crochet hook
- Cotton thread for hand sewing

Abbreviations
See page 78–79

To make
• Begin by crocheting the base. With the 3mm crochet hook and double-knit yarn, make 6ch then join with sl st.

Round 1: Work 12dc into circle, then join with sl st.

Round 2: Work 1ch *2dc in first st, 1dc in next. Repeat from * to end (18sts), joining with sl st at end.

Round 3: Work 1ch *2dc in first st, 1dc in each of following 2sts. Repeat from * to end (24sts), joining with a sl st.

Round 4: Work 1ch *2dc in first st, 1dc in each of following 3sts. Repeat from * to end (30sts), joining with a sl st.

• Continue crocheting as set, increasing on each round until the base is the correct diameter for your crochet bowl. For the bowls in the photograph we increased until round 4 for the small size, round 7 for the medium size and round 9 for the largest.

• Now build the walls of the bowl. **On the next round:** 1ch, work 1dc in each dc to end, join with a sl st.

• Continue until your work measures the appropriate height. Add extra rows if you want to make a turn-down cuff.

Last round (optional): Place the crochet hook between first and second dc (not into the top as on all previous rows) and make 1dc continue all around the row, ending with a sl st. This creates a double edge that will strengthen the top of your work.

• Sew in any loose ends and then fold down the top to the desired height.

Tips
You can use any thickness of yarn with the appropriate crochet hook to produce different-sized containers. A finer yarn will make a small container, while a thick yarn will produce a larger one. The pattern is flexible – make a wider base for a larger pot and a narrower base for a smaller one. Crochet fewer rows for a short pot and more for a taller one.

Decorated coat hangers

Knitted and crocheted coat hangers look good and their texture stops silky clothes from slipping off. They also make a lovely present, particularly if they are personalised with the recipient's name.

You will need

- 1 x 50g (2oz) ball 4-ply mercerised cotton (or matt cotton) for main colour (MC) (for the knitted cover)
- 2 x 25g (1oz) 4-ply mercerised cotton in contrasting colours (for the crocheted cover)
- 2.75mm (UK size 12; US size 2) knitting needles (for the knitted cover)
- 2mm and 2.25mm crochet hooks (for the crocheted cover and crochet flower)
- Wooden coat hangers
- Darning needle

Abbreviations
See pages 77 and 79

Measurements
45cm (18in) on top curve of coat hanger or 32cm (12½in) for child's coat hanger

Knitted coat-hanger cover
Cast on stitches the width of the hanger front and back, and knit in garter stitch until the length of the hanger has been reached.

Tension over garter stitch
26sts and 48 rows = 10cm (4in)

To make
• With 2.75mm (UK size 12; US size 2) needles and MC, cast on 17sts.

• Work in garter st (knit every row) until strip measures length of coat hanger when slightly stretched. Cast off.

• Find the centre of work in both length and width and slip over hanger hook.

• Stitch the strip together on the underside of the hanger with a neat catch st. Sew both ends to close.

To make the hook cover
• With 2.75mm (UK size 12; US size 2) needles and MC, cast on 38sts (measure your hanger hook and adjust accordingly). Work 4 rows in garter st. Cast off.

Fold around hook and sew edges together so the hook is covered. Catch to hanger cover to avoid hook cover slipping off. Alternatively, wrap the hook with the yarn, securing at each end with a blob of PVA glue.

Continues on page 65

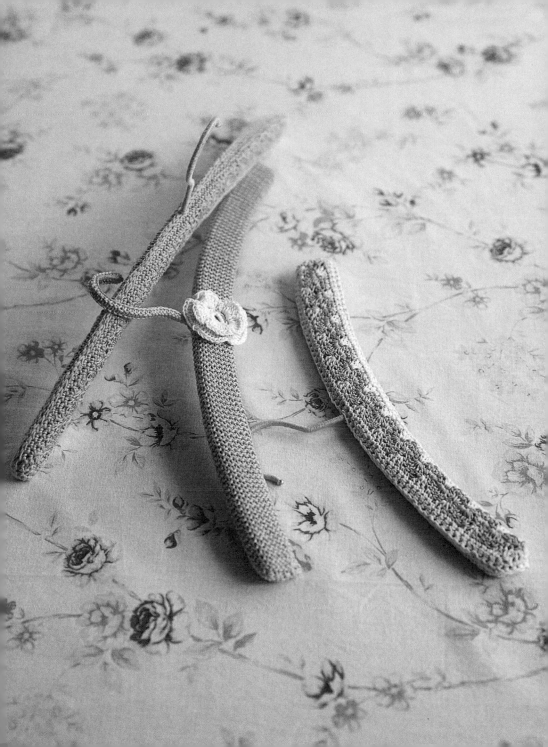

Crocheted coat hanger cover

This uses two colours of yarn in a textured pattern.

To make

• The shell pattern is made up of a multiple of 6ch plus 3 turning chain. So reduce or add by 6, depending on the length of your coat hanger.

This pattern is worked as 4 rows either side of the central 100 (76) chain with rows 5 and 6 worked all around the work.

• With the 2.25mm crochet hook and 4-ply yarn, make 100 (76)ch.

Row 1: Work 2tr in 4th chain from hook, * miss 2ch, 1dc in next ch, miss 2ch, 5tr in next ch. Repeat from * to end, finishing with 1dc in last chain.
Row 2: NB This row is worked along the base of chain. Sl st into side of last dc from row 1, then work 3ch, 2tr into first ch (where last dc from row 1 was made), * miss 2ch, 1dc (into chain where last group of 5tr were made on the previous row), miss 2ch, 5tr into next ch. Repeat from * to end, finishing with 1dc at end.
Row 3: Change colour, 3ch, 2tr on top of last dc from row 2, * 1dc either side of the centre treble of the 5tr cluster from row 2, 3tr in next dc. Repeat from * to end.
Row 4: Sl st down side of work and repeat row 3 above row 1.
Rows 5 & 6: Dc all around the edge of work. Fasten off.

To join: Place two pieces together, wrong sides facing. Sl st together along bottom edge and half of top. Then place onto the hanger and finish sl stitching together onto the hanger.

• Leave the hook bare or bind it using a length of the yarn, securing at each end with a blob of PVA glue.

Crocheted flower (optional)

• With the 2mm crochet hook and contrast colour, make 6ch and join with a sl st.

Row 1: Work 15dc into the circle, join with a sl st.
Row 2: 1ch, 1dc in first dc,* 3ch, 1dc into 3rd dc, repeat from*. End with 3ch then sl st to first dc.
Row 3: 1ch, work a petal of (1dc, 3ch, 5tr, 3ch, 1dc) into each of next five 3ch arches, sl st to first dc.
Row 4: 1ch (1dc between 2dc, 5ch behind petal of 3rd round) 5 times, sl st to first dc.
Rows 5: 1ch, work a petal of (1dc, 3ch, 7tr, 3ch, 1dc) into each of the five 5ch arches, sl st to first dc.

• Sew flower to centre of hanger.

Painted hangers

• To ensure a good finish, use a couple of coats of gloss paint in your chosen colour, and allow to dry completely before adding your design or name in a contrasting colour.

• Use as little paint as is needed to create an even coverage and flat finish. It will also keep drips to a minimum. When applying the background colour, paint the entire hanger and hang it on a clothesline (or similar) to dry, with newspaper beneath to catch any drips.

Crochet iPad cover

This is a great, practical way to make your iPad unique and its simple shape means it is easy to adapt for any tablet or e-Reader. The envelope-style button flap stops the gadget from falling out.

You will need

- 100g (3½oz) double knit (DK) cotton yarn
- 3.5mm crochet hook
- 1 button
- Darning needle

Abbreviations

See page 79

To make

- With a 3.5mm crochet hook and double-knit yarn, make 33ch, then turn.

Base row: Work 1tr into 4th chain from hook, then 1tr into all subsequent chain to end (30sts). Make 3 turning ch, then turn.
Row 1: Work 1tr in every stitch to end of row. Make 3 turning ch. * Repeat Row 1 until the work measures 50cm (19½in).
Next row: Tr next 2sts together, work to last 2 sts, tr next 2 sts together, make 3 turning ch. Repeat last row another 7 times.

To make up

- Fold your work in half, lining up the base row with the last row made before decreasing and pin in place.

- Beginning at the bottom right-hand corner, join your work together by working a row of dc up the first seam, around the envelope flap, and down the second seam to the bottom left-hand corner.

- Make 2ch, turn, then make another row of dc around your work. Break off the yarn, thread it through the last loop and sew in any loose ends.

To make the button loop

- Use a DK thread double (2 ends of DK), make a foundation chain that will fit around your chosen button – ours was 10ch for a 2cm (¾in) button.

- Sew both ends to the centre of the envelope flap using a darning needle.

- Using the same yarn and darning needle, sew a button onto the case.

For a tablet or e-Reader

- To convert the pattern to your device, you need to make a tension swatch. Start by making a 10cm chain plus 3 turning ch.

Base row: Work 1tr into 4th chain from hook and all subsequent chain to end, make 3 turning ch (12sts). Turn.
Row 1: Work 1tr in every stitch to the end of the row. Make 3 turning ch.
Repeat Row 1 until your work measures 10cm (4in).

- Count how many sts and rows you have per 10cm (½in) and average this out for 1cm (½in) and then measure the width and length of your device and use your 'stitches per cm/in' count to work out how many stitches you'll need for your own device. Follow the instructions for making an iPad cover but use the appropriate number of sts and length for your e-Reader.

Homemade basics

Craft basics

Whether it's making cushions or throws, wrapping presents or creating cards, having a well-stocked craft kit at the ready can help everything go smoothly. This section tells you what to save for recycling to quickly build the perfect vintage store cupboard.

Our craft kits are a combination of bought stuff – tried-and-tested glues, paints and other products that we know will work well – and goodies saved from here and there, happy in the knowledge that they will be given another life in some creative project or other. We save everything, from pretty wrapping paper (larger areas only and with the creases ironed out where necessary) to rubber bands and ribbons from presents or bouquets of flowers, and even the coloured cotton tape from the heavy paper bags that are increasingly given away in clothes and other shops instead of plastic bags. Not having to hunt around the house to locate the right type of glue, roll of sticky tape and so on will allow your creativity full rein, ensuring that your project will turn out the best it can possibly be, so these pages list a few suggestions for building a good, general craft kit.

Saving items for recycling can be problematic in terms of storage, but we've found that a large drawer works really well, especially when it contains boxes or dividers to keep everything organised. Also useful are mini chests of drawers made from wood or cardboard that can be stacked up alongside or on top of one another and added to when required. But as with the projects, be creative. You might prefer something more idiosyncratic to contain your kit, such as a sturdy reclaimed wicker laundry basket with old biscuit tins housing all the bits inside, or a series of lovely old leather suitcases of varying sizes. The important thing is to have a system that works efficiently and looks pleasing into the bargain.

The craft kit

- Different types of glue for paper, fabric and wood, and super-glue for fiddly items
- Sticky tape and double-sided tape
- Masking tape
- Roll of brown parcel paper
- Stick-on plain white labels of various sizes
- Lead pencils

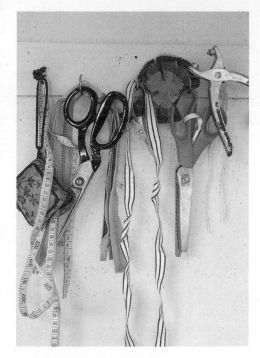

When it comes to giving away your handmade works of art, you'll want the wrapping to be just as special. Keep old magazines and a few newspapers, which can make great wrap, and always have a roll of wallpaper or lining paper on hand – these can be used to wrap any size object. Lining paper is the perfect blank canvas for painting, or decorating with flowers, feathers or pompoms, photographs or pictures from magazines.

Here are the basics we keep on hand for wrapping presents:

- Brown parcel paper
- Newsprint and magazine paper
- Lining paper (from a wallpaper or DIY store)
- Tissue paper in a variety of colours
- Rescued/reused wrapping paper sorted into larger pieces for reuse and smaller pieces for strips and borders (if you can find time to iron out creases, the paper will look much better)
- String
- Raffia
- Reels of new ribbon in one or two key colours. Red, for example, can perk up newsprint or brown paper and silver is good for use with tissue paper or even coloured magazine pages
- Gold and silver paints, which are good for painting stars, names and other adornments
- Silver and gold pens
- Pompoms and other embellishments
- Old-fashioned brown paper luggage labels in various sizes or scraps of cardboard for making your own labels
- Dried leaves and flowers

- Coloured crayons
- Set of felt pens
- Fountain pen and coloured inks
- Fabric paints and/or fabric crayons
- Staple gun
- Drawing pins
- Tacks
- Hammer
- Paper (coloured and white)
- Scissors (small and large)
- Pinking shears
- Ribbons
- Fabric scraps
- Yarn scraps
- Buttons
- Erasable pencil/chalk
- Brushes in various sizes, from 5–7.5cm (2–3in) to pointed artist's brushes

Sewing basics

This section tells you what kind of things to keep in your sewing kit, to make the projects from this book and anything else you're likely to want to sew. It also shows you how to sew the eight most useful stitches, and how to make a buttonhole.

It is good to have two sewing kits: one can be small and portable, containing the bare essentials (needles, thread, safety pins and a spare button or two) that you keep in a handbag and use for mending on the go, and the other much more extensive – based at home and used for larger projects, such as those in this book.

The following items are recommended for the larger kit.

The sewing kit
- At least two pairs of sharp scissors: small, very sharp embroidery scissors (good for unpicking) and a good-quality pair of fabric shears. By including both pairs of scissors, you are ensuring that the fabric scissors will last a long time.
- Pinking shears for making zigzag edges to hems (less likely to fray) and cutting fabrics, such as felt, in an attractive way.
- Pins stuck in an attractive pincushion, handmade if possible (see pages 52–53), though magnetic pin holders are also available. Many people find quilting pins with coloured heads easier to handle, and they are certainly easier to see, making it

less likely that you will leave pins in place on a finished item. Larger-headed pins are particularly useful when working with knitting or crochet.
- Hand-sewing needles in various sizes, including thicker darning needles for working with thicker thread or wool.
- Safety pins, fastened together for safety and convenience.
- Tailor's chalk for marking out patterns (this washes or brushes out easily).
- Cotton thread in various colours; keep commonly used colours in longer reels.
- Tape measure in imperial and metric.
- Poppers and hooks and eyes for fastening.
- Fusible fabric, such as Bondaweb.
- Button box containing buttons of all shapes, colours and sizes.
- Rag bag full of scraps and smaller pieces of fabric that you have saved up over the years.
- Steam iron for pressing fabric before, during and after making up.

Non-essentials, but useful
- Basic sewing machine (not essential but certainly useful) and a variety of sewing machine needles.
- Thimble, especially if you get sore fingers and thumbs.
- Seam ripper/unpicker.
- Ruler to provide a more solid edge than a tape measure.
- Embroidery threads in all colours.
- Tapestry wool for embellishments.

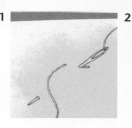  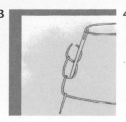 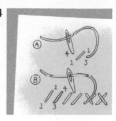

Basic stitches used in this book

Most of the instructions below and overleaf are based on those supplied on the website of the Embroiderer's Guild (www.embroiderersguild.com/stitch/ stitches). There are also some superb YouTube entries, some of which show the creation of the stitches very clearly, accompanied by music.

1 Back stitch

Bring the thread up through the fabric on the stitch line and then take a small backward stitch down through the fabric. Bring the needle through again a little in front of the first stitch, then take another backwards stitch, inserting the needle at the point where it first came through.

2 Blanket stitch

Push the needle up through the fabric a short way from the edge, hooking the rest of the thread around the top of the needle. Pull the needle through the fabric, keeping the lower thread out of the way so the thread forms a loop around the edge of the fabric. Repeat to create a line of linked stitches along the fabric edge.

3 Chain stitch

Having pulled the needle through the fabric, insert the needle next to where it emerged and bring the point out a short distance away. Pull the thread around the needle, keeping it under the needle's point, and pull the needle through the fabric to create a looped stitch. Holding down the loop, repeat to make a series of linked chains.

4 Cross stitch

Working on the canvas holes in groups of four, bring the needle up through the lower left hole (1) and take it down through the canvas one hole up and to the right (2). Bring it through to the front again one hole down (3) to form a half cross. Continue in this way to the end of the row, then complete the upper section of the cross. Cross stitch can be worked from left to right, as shown, or from right to left, but it is important that the upper half of each cross lies in one direction.

Continues on page 74

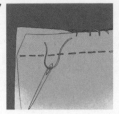
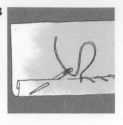

5 Hem stitch

Fold the hem horizontally with your thumb on the hem. Lay the end of your thread in the fold of the hem. Working from left to right, take a small back stitch through just the hem to anchor the thread. Moving a small way along the fabric to the right, pick up two threads from the work and pull gently. Then pick up two threads from the folded hem, to the right of the first stitch. Move on to the next two threads in the work, pull gently and then pick up two threads in the hem. Continue working in this way until the whole item is hemmed.

6 Running stitch

Pass the needle in and out of the fabric, making sure that the surface stitches are of equal length. The stitches on the underside should be of equal length to one another, but half the size or less than the upper stitches.

7 Over stitch

This stitch is worked from the right side and is often used to join together pieces of fabric, or as an alternative to blanket stitch to prevent fraying. Place the pieces of work together with wrong sides facing, then bring the needle up through both layers from the underside. Repeat, always bringing the needle from the underside of the work.

The thread binds together the two layers of fabric. Over stitch is especially useful for joining the fabric of a stuffed toy.

8 Slip stitch

A slip stitch can be used to repair a seam from the top. Push a threaded needle (be sure to knot the thread) through the material on one side of the opening, and then on the other. Continue until the seam is closed.

Making a buttonhole

These instructions tell you how to make a buttonhole using any sewing machine that can make a zigzag. If you have a newer machine, with fancy pre-programmed buttonhole settings, you don't need to do it this way. Or you can handstitch by sewing around the open hole initially using over stitch and then buttonhole stitch, which is basically blanket stitch worked very closely together (see page 73). Neatly done, a hand-sewn buttonhole is a work of art. Most buttonholes are made with thread that matches the fabric colour. Stick to that convention for any machine-sewn buttonholes, as no matter how well these are done they will be functional rather than decorative. For buttonholes beautiful enough to be a feature, hand-sewn or bound buttonholes are the answer.

- Mark out your buttonholes with tailor's chalk. They should be at least 5mm (¼in) larger than the buttons you intend to use. As a rule, buttonholes should be parallel with the edge of the garment so the button will pull on the end of the buttonhole, not the middle, where it would gape and look strange. The traditional marking is shaped like a capital 'I', which emphasises where the ends are so all of the buttonholes end up the same length.

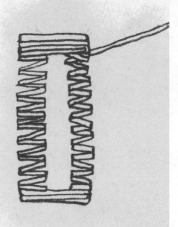

- On the sewing machine, set your stitch width to maximum and your stitch length to zero to create a wide zigzag that isn't going anywhere fast.

- Position the needle at the furthest end of the buttonhole marking. Stitch five or six zigzags to create the bar at that end of the buttonhole, finishing with your needle on the left. (Don't pull the fabric out or cut the thread after this stage – you want the thread to be taut between steps.)

- Set the stitch width to half of the maximum value and increase the stitch length a little. Stitch down the length of the buttonhole to the other end. Once again, don't pull the fabric out or cut the thread after this stage.

- Reset your stitch width to maximum and your stitch length to zero. Reposition the needle so its centre position matches the centre line of the buttonhole.

- Make five or seven zigzags at that end of the buttonhole. Be sure to do an odd

number, so you end up with the needle at the extreme right. Leave the needle down and turn the entire garment around by 180 degrees.

- Once again, set the stitch width to half the maximum value and increase the stitch length a tiny bit. Position the needle so that its leftmost position matches the leftmost extent of the stitching just completed.

- Stitch down the length of the buttonhole back to where you started, being careful to stay parallel to the first side you sewed. Let the zigzag go a little into the starting zigzag for added strength.

- Using either buttonhole scissors, a seam unpicker or ordinary sewing scissors, carefully cut open the buttonhole. Make sure you don't cut the stitching, particularly at the ends. Snip any loose threads and try passing the button through the hole.

Knitting basics

One of the best things about knitting is that you need very little in the way of equipment, especially when knitting simple items such as gloves and scarves. The real skill lies in choosing yarns and getting to know your preferred style and tension.

By far the best way to learn knitting is one-on-one from a more experienced friend or relative. But there are also many groups and drop-in 'clinics' around, both formal and informal, where the sociable side of craft also comes into play. For further information on courses, see the Directory on pages 86–91. The excellent website www.domiknitrix.com includes a gallery of pictures to help you learn various stitches, including mattress stitch.

The knitting kit
- A selection of knitting needles: the ones used in this book are size 2.75mm (UK size 12; US size 2), 3.25mm (UK size 10; US size 3), 4.5mm (UK size 7; US size 7) and 6.5mm (UK size 3; US size 10½).
- Various crochet hooks of different sizes, including 2mm and 2.5mm.
- Tape measure.
- Small sharp scissors.
- Pencil and paper.
- Stitch holder (at least one, for holding stitches when changing needles).
- Safety pins of various sizes.
- Needle gauge: for checking needle sizes.
- Circular needles: for making socks and gloves.
- Darning needles: for sewing flat pieces of knitting together.
- Button box of buttons.
- Selection of small scraps of knitting yarn for embroidery and darning.

Choosing yarn
Different yarns give different results: smooth and silky or rough and hairy. Long filaments create a different effect compared to short ones – compare the difference between an item made with mohair and one made with a tightly twisted yarn. Take this into account when choosing yarn for a project.

Whatever yarn you choose, try to make it the best possible quality. After all the time and love you put into making something, you don't want it to look tired, misshapen and bobbly after only one wash. Numerous companies (see the Directory, pages 86–91) make beautiful ranges of pure and mixed yarn and have pure wool that washes well and feels soft and wearable.

Yarn usually comes in 50g (2oz) balls but, for economy, try to find yarn on large hanks, or larger still 500g (1lb 2oz) cones, which are a cheaper option when buying new.

Quite often yarn is reduced if it is an odd dye lot (see 'Notes for knitters', right) and this is worth buying to add to your store when knitting or crocheting things that use small quantities, such as the Crochet squares (see page 56), Decorated coat hangers (see page 62), Fingerless gloves (see page 16) and Tea cosy (see page 10).

The make-do-and-mend mentality of the post-war generation meant it was common for people to unravel and re-knit their jerseys, steaming the wool to take out the kinks. While we wouldn't advocate this as essential, it certainly makes sense financially, provided you have time. It might be worth considering the next time your child outgrows a favourite hand-knit or you see an item made from a lovely yarn but don't like the garment style.

Knitting terms

In the UK and USA, yarns are referred to by different terms:

UK	US
4-ply	Sportweight
Double knit	Worsted
Aran	Fisherman or medium weight
Chunky	Bulky

Notes for knitters

- ALWAYS work a tension swatch, no matter how little time you have. Then check it against the pattern and change your needles accordingly if necessary.
- The knitting and crochet tensions quoted on all the patterns in this book are a guide only. Every knitter has a natural personal tension, which may be tight or loose.
- To check your tension, knit a square to the size given in the pattern and using the stitch from the pattern. When the square is complete, lay it on a flat surface and, using a tape measure, count the number of stitches and then the number of rows.

- If you have more stitches or rows than the tension indicated, use slightly smaller needles. If you have fewer stitches or rows, try using larger needles.
- The difference in tension also means that some knitters may use more or less yarn than that quoted. Once you know whether your tension is slightly tight or loose, adjust your yarn allowance slightly.
- If buying more than one ball of the same-coloured yarn, make sure they all have the same batch number – this is printed on the ball band. Although balls of yarn may look the same to the naked eye, the same colour from different dye batches will always show on the finished piece and spoil the uniform effect.
- When it's time to put your knitting away, pop a cork on the end of needles to stop the stitches falling off.
- Never leave your knitting in the middle of a row or there may be an obviously larger stitch in the middle once it is finished.

Abbreviations used for the projects

cont	continue
col	colour
dec	decrease/decreasing
inc	increase/increasing
k	knit
MC	main colour
p	purl
rep	repeat
RS	right side
st/sts	stitches
tog	together

Crochet basics

In Victorian times, crochet was used extensively for making and decorating clothes and household items. Its resurgence in popularity today owes much to the qualities those Victorians admired: it creates pretty but long-lasting, hard-wearing items. It's also much easier to learn than you would think, and kids love it.

Just as with knitting, there are lots of different crochet stitches that can vary the look and texture of your work. Just Google 'how to crochet' and you'll find thousands of websites packed with advice and able to teach you everything you need to get started.

The crochet kit

- A selection of crochet hooks of different sizes. The ones used in this book are 2mm and 2.5mm.
- Tape measure: ideally a retractable one in an attractive case.
- Small sharp scissors: embroidery scissors are ideal.
- Pencil and paper: for notes and making impromptu patterns.
- Stitch holder: at least one – for holding stitches when changing hooks.
- Safety pins of various sizes.
- Darning needles: for sewing together flat pieces of crochet.
- Buttons.
- Selection of small scraps of knitting yarn for embroidery or darning: these can be kept in a pretty tin.

Your crochet kit will probably fit into a fairly small box, bag or tin. Whether you choose a zip-up or closed-hinge receptacle rather than an open one depends largely on whether you will be taking your kit out with you (on the bus or train or even to the cinema), or keeping it at home, and whether you need to keep your work and yarn protected from the ravages of children and/or pets. Choose something attractive, though, which will help you keep your work in order and make you want to pick it up often.

Choosing yarn

Traditionally, crochet yarn is a fine cotton, tightly twisted to avoid splitting. It gives a firmer finish to your work than other yarns, which was important for household objects crocheted from mid-1800 to around 1950, and those produced today by artisans in some European and South American countries. The yarn is still available and is usually referred to as 'crochet cotton'. This fine cotton is best suited to lace work and – unless you are working from a vintage pattern, making something like traditional table linens (hardly likely if you are a beginner) – is far too fine for contemporary patterns and styles.

Although you may be making small crochet flowers in the traditional manner, working from a contemporary colour palette would make them into incredibly fashionable accessories. There's a pattern for a simple crochet flower on page 65.

Some people use knitting yarns in all crochet work requiring thicker yarns. It is vital that the yarn you choose is appropriate for the design and that you avoid anything knobbly or with a slub, as these cause problems when working stitches together – and this commonly happens in crochet patterns. See also Knitting basics (pages 76–77).

Crochet terms

European and US stitches are the same, but other crochet terms differ.

UK	US
Cast off	Fasten off
Double crochet (dc)	Single crochet (sc)
Double treble	Treble (tr)
Miss	Skip
Tension	Gauge
Treble (tr)	Double crochet (dc)
Work straight	Work even

Abbreviations used in this book

ch	chain
dc	double crochet
sl st	slip stitch
sp	space
tr	treble

Hook sizes

Crochet hooks are made from aluminium, plastic, bamboo or sometimes even bone. European and US hook sizes differ and since 1970 they have been given as listed in the column opposite. For a look at some fascinating, pre-1970 hooks, visit www.antiquepatternlibrary.org

Steel hooks

mm range	US range*
0.75mm	14
0.85mm	13
1mm	12
1.1mm	11
1.3mm	10
1.4mm	9
1.5mm	8
1.65mm	7
1.8mm	6
1.9mm	5
2mm	4
2.1mm	3
2.25mm	2
2.75mm	1
3.25mm	0
3.5mm	00

Aluminum hooks

mm range	US range*
2.25mm	B-1
2.75mm	C-2
3.25mm	D-3
3.5mm	E-4
3.75mm	F-5
4mm	G-6
4.5mm	7
5mm	H-8
5.5mm	I-9
6mm	J-10
6.5mm	K-101/2
8mm	L-11
9mm	M/N-13
10mm	N/P-15
15mm	P/Q
16mm	Q
19mm	S

* The letter or number may vary, so rely on the millimetre (mm) sizing.

Patterns and templates

The patterns we have used are very simple and, in most cases, consist of a hard outline with a dotted line if there is a seam allowance or a line of stitching. Follow the instructions for how many pieces to cut and where material needs to be doubled and/or placed on a fold. In some instances there are other markings that need to be transferred such as seam allowances and button and buttonhole positions. Provided the pattern does not need sizing up, trace the outline plus any other detailing onto tracing paper. Pin the paper onto the fabric and cut around the fabric, cutting through the paper too, if this is the first time you have used the pattern. Transfer any extra markings to the fabric using dressmaker's chalk, which will wash out.

Egg cosies

See project on pages 46–47
Enlarge pattern to 140% to reach size required

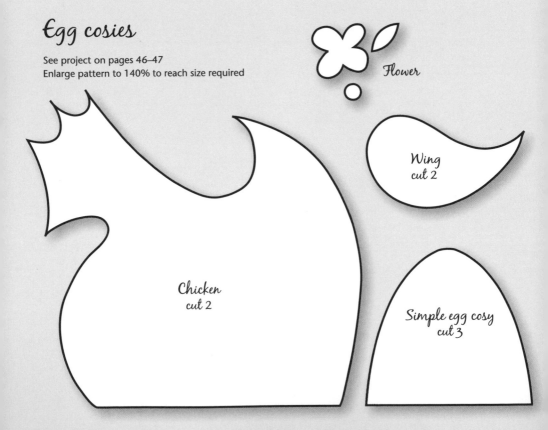

Flower

Wing
cut 2

Chicken
cut 2

Simple egg cosy
cut 3

Lavender cats

See project on pages 50–51

Enlarge pattern to 140% to reach actual size required

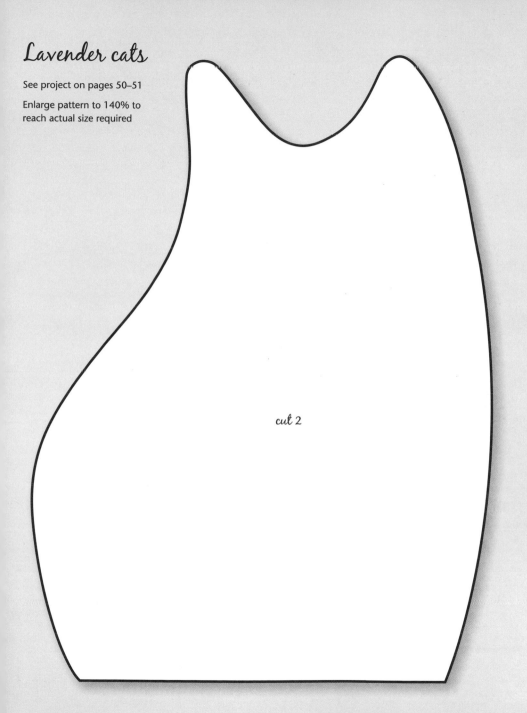

cut 2

Child's summer dress

See project on pages 30–33

Enlarge pattern to 265%
to reach actual size required

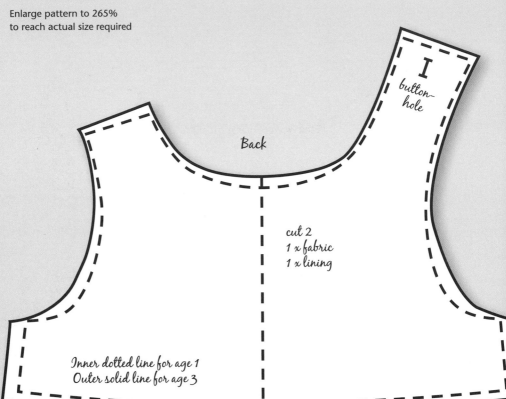

Back

I
button-
hole

cut 2
1 x fabric
1 x lining

Inner dotted line for age 1
Outer solid line for age 3

Side straps   cut 2

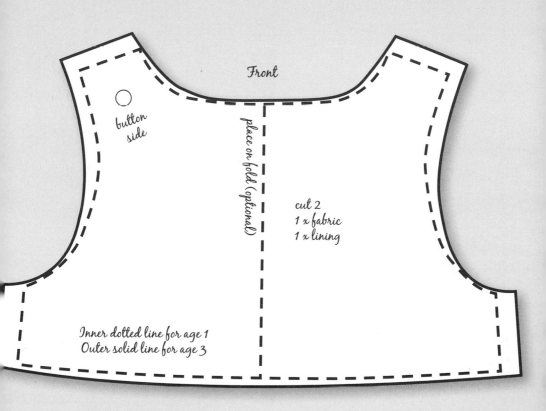

Front

button
side

place on fold (optional)

cut 2
1 x fabric
1 x lining

Inner dotted line for age 1
Outer solid line for age 3

place on fold

Age 1

Age 3

Continues on page 84

top

gather to 2cm (¾in) from edge

←

Child's summer dress
Skirt

Front and Back

cut 2
Inner dotted line for age 1
Outer solid line for age 3

place on fold

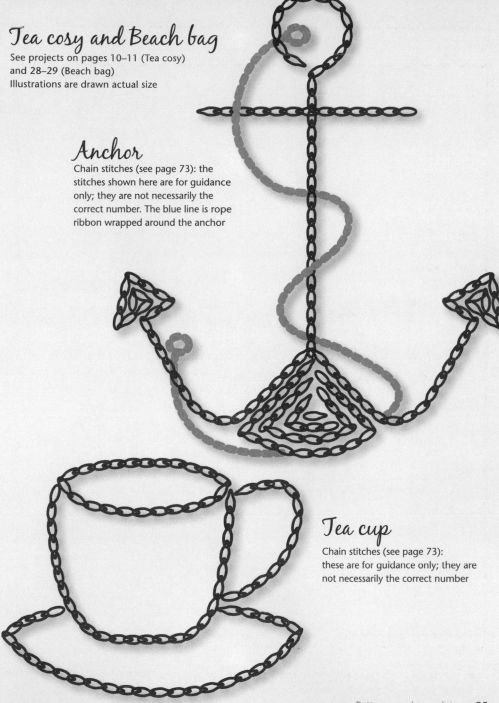

Tea cosy and Beach bag

See projects on pages 10–11 (Tea cosy)
and 28–29 (Beach bag)
Illustrations are drawn actual size

Anchor

Chain stitches (see page 73): the
stitches shown here are for guidance
only; they are not necessarily the
correct number. The blue line is rope
ribbon wrapped around the anchor

Tea cup

Chain stitches (see page 73):
these are for guidance only; they are
not necessarily the correct number

Directory

Sewing

Useful organisations

Northern Ireland Embroidery Guild
www.nieg.org.uk
No address given, but excellent workshops in embroidery, felting and beadwork.

Royal School of Needlework
Apartment 12A,
Hampton Court Palace,
East Molesey, Surrey KT8 9AU
T 020 3166 6932
www.royal-needlework.co.uk
Charity whose mission is to teach, practise and promote the art of hand embroidery to the highest standards, within both historical and contemporary design contexts. Offers a variety of courses for beginners to highly experienced needleworkers, including one-day courses and year-long training. Tours of their inspiring collection of needlework through the ages and of their studio are also available – all in the genteel surroundings of Hampton Court Palace.

Sewing shops and mail-order suppliers

The Cloth House
47 Berwick Street,
London W1F 8SJ
T 020 7437 5155
www.clothhouse.com
Vintage trimmings and ribbons alongside a huge range of natural fabrics.

The Cloth Shop
290 Portobello Road,
London W10 5TE
T 020 8968 6001
www.theclothshop.net

The Cotton Patch
1285 Stratford Road, Hall Green, Birmingham B28 9AJ
T 0121 702 2840
www.cottonpatch.co.uk
Fantastic shop and website specialising in patchwork fabrics and accessories.

Duttons for Buttons
Oxford Street, Harrogate,
North Yorkshire HG1 1QE
T 01423 502 092
www.duttonsforbuttons.co.uk
Wonderful shop bursting with all manner of buttons and haberdashery. Supplies by mail order. See website for other outlets.

Exeter Sewing Machine Company
7 Heavitree Road, Exeter,
Devon EX1 2LD
T 01392 275 660
www.exetersewing.co.uk
Great source of thread, fabric and general supplies for avid seamstresses.

I Knit London
106 Lower Marsh, Waterloo,
London SE1 7AB
T 020 7261 1338
www.iknit.org.uk

In-Fabrics
12 Old Bridge,
Haverfordwest,
Pembrokeshire SA61 2ET
T 01437 769 164

www.in-fabrics.com
More than 2,000 rolls of
fabric in stock!

Kleins
5 Noel Street,
London W1F 8GD
T 020 7437 6162
www.kleins.co.uk
Chaos reigns in this Soho
institution, but chances are
they will have what you want
… plus they do mail order.

Lady Sew and Sew
Moy House, 57 Institute
Road, Marlow, Bucks SL7 1BN
T 01628 890 532
www.ladysewandsew.com
Fabric shop selling quilting,
haberdashery and sewing kits.

Liberty
Regent Street,
London W1B 5AH
T 020 7734 1234
www.liberty.co.uk
This huge, wonderful shop
is an all-time classic – its
olde worlde appearance
belies its very up-to-date
and stylish stock – both the
haberdashery and furnishing
departments are brilliant, and
very inspiring.

MacCulloch and Wallis
25–26 Dering Street,
London W1S 1AT
T 020 7629 0311

www.macculloch-wallis.co.uk
Old-fashioned fabric shop
selling all sorts of dress
trimmings and materials, as
well as good haberdashery
supplies.

Mandors
131 East Claremont Street,
Edinburgh EH7 4JA
T 0131 558 3888
www.mandors.co.uk
Mandors have a great supply
of dressmaking and furnishing
materials.

Millie Moon Shop
24–25 Catherine Hill,
Frome, Somerset BA11 1BY
T 01373 464 650
www.milliemoonshop.co.uk
Haberdashery boutique and
sewing school.

Millers Creativity Shop
28 Stockwell Street,
Glasgow G1 4RT
T 0141 553 1660
www.millers-art.co.uk
Creative superstore with
plenty of sewing equipment.

Olicana Textiles Ltd
Brook Mills, Crimble,
Slaithwaite, Huddersfield HD7
T 01484 847 666

Sew Creative
97–99 King Street,
Cambridge CB1 1LD

T 01223 350 691
www.sewcreative.co.uk
Suppliers of Pfaff and Singer
sewing machines along
with a good range of yarn
and fabric.

The Sewing Bee
52 Hillfoot Street, Dunoon,
Argyll, Scotland PA23 7DT
T 01369 706 879
www.thesewingbee.co.uk
Gorgeous bijou haberdashers.

**Singer and Pfaff Sewing
Centre**
2 Queen Street, Penzance,
Cornwall TR18 4BJ
T 01736 363 457
www.iriss.co.uk
Supplier of sewing machines
with a good range of fabrics.

Samuel Taylor
10 Central Road,
Leeds LS1 6DE
T 0113 245 9737
www.clickoncrafts.co.uk
Old-fashioned haberdasher
that has a great modern
online shop.

St Jude's Fabrics
T 01603 662 951
www.stjudesfabrics.co.uk
St Jude's works with an
eclectic range of artists to
produce original printed
fabrics that form a brilliant
basis for almost anything.

VV Rouleaux
www.vvrouleaux.com
Famous ribbon specialists
with fabulous selection in
many colours and widths.
See website for branches in
England and Scotland.

Sewing websites

www.betsyrosspatterns.com
Easy-to-follow sewing
patterns that can be ordered
online.

www.ciaspalette.com
Well-chosen selection of
quilting fabrics with a
personal touch from
Cia herself.

www.clothkits.co.uk
The original 1970s designs
reworked for today in those
trademark 'cut out and snip
to size' patterns.

www.equilter.com
Fabrics for sale, plus 'design
board' feature that allows you
to try them out in thumbnail
samples.

www.fitzpatterns.com
Fashionably funky patterns to
download, many for free.

www.gloriouscolor.com
American quilter's site that
ships internationally.

www.jkneedles.com
Materials and accessories
for all kinds of needlework,
including beginners' kits
and DVDs.

www.opheliabutton.co.uk
Jewellery and other treasures
made from beautiful vintage
buttons.

www.sewessential.co.uk
Range of haberdashery and
sewing supplies.

www.sewing.org
Instructions on a wide
range of techniques,
including fashion sewing
and creating pet clothes.

www.sewmamasew.com
Gorgeous and fun modern
cotton fabrics and patterns
from indie designers in
Oregon, USA.

www.vpll.org
Fascinating pattern library
featuring designs from
1840 to 1950 with vintage
publications too.

Sewing books

Colourful Stitchery by Kristin
Nicholas (Storey Books).
Wonderful, exuberant
embroidery that is sure to
inspire and delight.

*Mary Thomas's Dictionary of
Embroidery Stitches* by Mary
Thomas (Caxton Editions).
A real classic.

Knitting and crochet

Useful organisations

Knitting and Crochet Guild
www.kcguild.org.uk
An amazing organisation
set up to promote and
encourage the crafts of
hand knitting, machine
knitting and crochet. Aimed
at makers that are also
interested in the history of
knitting and crochet, it is
full of information and links
to archival material. It runs
classes too.

UK Hand Knitting
Association
www.ukhandknitting.com
A mine of information on
classes, knitting groups,
shows and shops.

Victoria and Albert Museum
Cromwell Road,
London SW7 2RL
T 020 7942 2000
www.vam.ac.uk
Has a great website – type
'knitting' into the seach
box for everything from the

history of knitting to the best shops, free patterns and knitting blogs.

Knitting and crochet classes

Learning from other people is the best way to start any new craft – either one-on-one with a friend or in a group of local people interested in extending their skills. There are also various 'knitting gurus' offering tailor-made classes for individuals or groups. And don't forget YouTube!

Ros Badger, one of the authors of this book, offers knitting lessons in South London (www.rosbadger. com) and her book *Instant Expert: Knitting* is full of inspirational photographs. See her blog at www.rosbadger.blogspot. co.uk and follow her on Twitter: @rosbadger.

Knitting shops and mail-order suppliers

Get Knitted
39 Brislington Hill, Brislington, Bristol BS4 5BE
www.getknitted.com
Great yarns and patterns.

Loop
15 Camden Passage, London N1 8EA
T 020 7288 1160
www.loopknitting.com
Fine-looking shop stuffed with lovely candy-coloured yarns. You can also drop in for emergency knitting advice or enrol in lunchtime classes.

Purlescence Ltd
Boston House, Downsview Road, Wantage, Oxfordshire OX12 9YF
www.purlescence.co.uk
Purlescence has a modern take on all things knitting.

Stash Yarns
213 Upper Richmond Road, London SW15 6SQ
T 020 8246 6666
www.stashyarns.co.uk
Another great shop selling yarns from around the world.

Knitting websites

www.angelyarns.com
This site claims to be Europe's largest online yarn store, and it certainly does have a huge number of yarns!

www.castoff.info
Radical knitting website that arranges adventurous knitting meetings and workshops in unusual public settings.

www.colinette.com
An unusual range of hand-dyed yarns in many different colour combinations.

www.cornishorganicwool.co.uk
This company produces organically certified yarns, in pure wool and a wool/alpaca mix. All the wool is spun in Scotland at a mill powered by a water wheel and hand dyed.

www.domiknitrix.com
For no-nonsense, straight-talking help on knocking your knitting into shape – this site is as funny as it is informative.

www.kangaroo.uk.com
This site provides a world-wide mail-order service for knitting kits, patterns, yarns and needles.

www.knitty.com
An amazing US-based resource for knitters, offering free patterns, articles and technical advice for novices and experienced knitters alike – all spooled out with welcome warmth and humour in an online periodical magazine format.

www.laughinghens.com
Online wool store with a really good range of patterns, yarns (including organic), threads, kits, accessories and books.

www.louet.com
This US firm produces finest-quality Euroflax linen in an inspiring range of colours. They also sell exotic fibres, from Yak to silk.

www.shetland-wool-brokers.zetnet.co.uk

www.mazzmatazz.co.uk
Site of the original 'rebel knitter' who designed cuddly versions of *Doctor Who* villains along with other weird and wonderful stuff.

www.nexstitch.com
Easy-to-read crochet patterns for ponchos, shawls and other accessories – even bikinis.

www.ravelry.com
Like Facebook for knitters – you can share projects, tips and chat with like-minded fellow knitters.

www.simplysockyarn.com
American company with a great list of yarns from all the top producers.

www.stitchnbitch.org
For local group knitting and general craft-club gossip while you knit, or look at your local press and craft/art shop windows. Stitchnbitch also produce books with fun, unusual patterns.

www.texere.co.uk
All kinds of yarn, plus chenille, metallic yarns and embroidery thread.

www.theknittinghut.com

www.yarnstorm.co.uk
The wonderful website of Jane Brocket, who really put sewing, knitting and patchwork back on the map. Her book, *The Gentle Art of Domesticity,* is also a delight.

www.ysolda.com
Website of lovely young Scottish knitter.

Knitting books

Complete Guide to Knitting and Crochet by Nicki Trench (Parragon).
Great illustrations and an informative, easy-to-follow style of writing. The book includes plenty of simple but interesting projects that even beginners can master.

The Crochet Answer Book by Edie Eckman (Storey).
A useful addition to your crochet library.

Kyuuto! Japanese Crafts: Lacy Crochet (Chronicle Books).
Quirky patterns with a Japanese view on crochet.

General sites and suppliers

Some of these are places where we buy items we love, others (the more expensive among them) are where we go to get inspired. Exposing yourself to as much good-quality and beautiful material, whether it is clothes or furniture or food, is great for getting the mind going and thinking of your own ideas to create. It's not plagiarism – slavish copying is definitely not on the agenda – it's more letting one person's ideas and creativity inspire your own.

Mary Mathieson
An artist with a special interest in working with flowers, who did some of the illustrations and made many of the projects in this book. She can be contacted on **T 07940 919 622.**

www.caravanstyle.com
Stylist Emily Chalmers set up this gorgeous shop specialising in vintage thrift in the most stylish way possible.

www.charlenemullen.com
Incredibly talented textile designer specialising in cushions and homeware – rather expensive, but handmade using the most sumptuous fabrics and a real inspiration.

www.designspongeonline.com
Lovely things noticed and described with an observant and original eye.

www.etsy.com
The place to sell all your homemade craft items, to keen buyers from around the world.

www.frankworks.eu
British alternative applied arts and contemporary craft – books and badges, jewellery and stationery, textiles, prints, ceramics and lighting that are often handmade, original, quirky or downright eccentric.

www.fredbare.co.uk
For some of the most stylish hats in town. The lovely shop at 118 Columbia Road, London E2 7RG (01904 624 579) is usually only open on Sundays so ring or email via the website.

www.helpyourshelf.co.uk
Lovely website and shop full of unique and stylish objects.

www.vialiivia.blogspot.co.uk
You don't need to speak Finnish to appreciate this photographer's blog with its sensitive, beautiful photographs, documenting the homely (and naturally stylish) domestic life of Liivian and her young daughter. Her fellow Scandinavian's blog, Vintage Living at www.myblogvintageliving.blogspot.com, is similarly inspiring.

www.papastour.com
Scottish arts and crafts with lots of lovely things plus a hideaway to rent.

www.pedlars.co.uk
Great, fun, original items, including many that aid creativity – old printers' blocks, vintage tins and reclaimed plant pots, old-fashioned cleaning equipment, sticky tape dispensers and so on.

www.re-foundobjects.co.uk
'Re' stands for 'recycled, restored, reused' – and their website and shop are bristling with original finds and new ways to use old objects and fabrics, which can't help but be inspiring. Their store is in Bishops Yard, Main Street, Corbridge, Northumberland NE45 5LA.

www.squintlimited.com
For heavenly, somewhat pricey original items. Great for inspiring your own homespun versions.

www.yarnstorm.blogs.com
The creation of the fantastically inspiring and prolific Jane Brocket, who knits, patchworks, cooks and gardens and posts her creations online. This is one of the first and best of the many craft websites, including knitting, sewing, embroidery and patchwork as well as cake baking.

Index

hot-water bottle cover 48
unravelling 77

K

knitting 76–7
  abbreviations 77
  decorated coat hangers 62
  fingerless gloves 16–19
  iPod cover 8
  knitting kit 74
  striped woolly scarf 15
  tea cosy 10, 85
  tension swatches 77
  terms 77
  yarn 74–5

L

lavender
  drying 51
  lavender cats 51, 81

M

Mathieson, Mary 51
MP3 cover 8

N

needle gauges 74
needles
  darning needles 74, 78
  knitting needles 74
  sewing needles 72
'no-entry' sign, cross-stitch 55

O

outdoor cushion 38
over stitch 74

P

paper, wrapping gifts 71
patchwork
  crochet squares 56–9
  patchwork throw 34
pincushion, Victorian sand 52
pinking shears 72

pins 72
pompoms 12
poppers 72

Q

quilting pins 72

R

rulers 72
running stitch 74

S

safety pins 72, 74, 78
sand pincushion, Victorian 52
scarf, striped woolly 15
scissors 72, 74, 78
seam rippers 72
sewing 72–5
  bag-in-a-bag 24–7
  beach bag 28, 85
  buttonholes 74–5
  child's summer dress 30–3,
    82–4
  cross-stitch 'no-entry' sign 55
  cushion covers 37
  denim chair 41
  egg cosies 47, 80
  felt flower hair clips and combs
    20
  flower corsage 23
  hot-water bottle cover 48
  lavender cats 51, 81
  outdoor cushion 38
  patchwork throw 34
  sewing kit basics 72
  stitches 73–4
  summer bunting 42
  tea towel apron 44
  Victorian sand pincushion 52
sewing machines 72
slip stitch 74
squares, crochet 56–9
steam irons 72
stitch holders 74, 78

stitches, sewing 73–4
striped woolly scarf 15
summer bunting 42

T

tablet, crochet cover 67
tailor's chalk 72
tape measures 72, 74, 78
tapestry wool 72
tea cosy 10, 85
tea towel apron 44
templates 80–4
tension swatches 77
thimbles 72
threads
  cotton 72
  embroidery 72
throw, patchwork 34

V

Victorian sand pincushion 52

W

wool
  knitting yarn 74
  tapestry wool 72
wrapping gifts 71

Y

yarn
  batch numbers 77
  crochet 78–9
  knitting 74–5

Acknowledgements

I would like to thank my husband Benjamin J Murphy for his perfectionist's eye and dedication – his photographs have made this book truly beautiful. Also Mary Mathieson for her wonderful illustrations, and for contributing to various projects throughout the book. Hanks (sic) also to my very creative teenage daughters for their advice and quirkiness.

Huge thanks are also due to Jane Turnbull, a brilliant agent, who believed in this idea from the start; Denise Bates for the original commission and all at HarperCollins for their hard work, particularly Elen Jones for championing this new edition. Thanks to Sarah Tomley for her excellent editing skills, Rosie Scott for the clever templates and Tracy Killick for designing such a beautiful book.

I would also like to thank Piers Feltham, Chiara Menage, and Caddy and Chris Wilmot-Sitwell for allowing us to take photographs in their gardens.

Thank you also to the many other people who have contributed with their own imaginative ideas to this book – Monica McMillan, Katy Jaffey, Rebecca Tanqueray, Caddy Wilmot-Sitwell and Kristin Perers among others. Also to all the children who have travelled through my sewing clubs and who continue to inspire me with their never-ending inventive interpretations of my ideas.

Thank you to my mum Ruth Badger for teaching me how to sew when I was very young, and her sister Joan Kenwright who, together with my mum, spent hours 'on the sewing machine' throughout my childhood. Also thanks to my grandmother Mary Elizabeth Hunter for teaching me how to crochet when I was seven years old.

Lastly, to my dearest friend Elspeth Thompson whose reputation as a writer and all-round dedication to artistry meant we were commissioned to make *Homemade: Gorgeous Things to Make with Love* back in 2008. Her influence, vision and beauty will stay with me always.

Ros Badger